Tolu' A. Akinyemi

never play games with the devil

First published in Great Britain as a softback original in 2019

Copyright © Tolu' A. Akinyemi
The moral right of this author has been asserted.
All rights reserved.

No part of this publication may be reproduced, stored in a retrieval system, or transmitted, in any form or by any means, without the prior permission in writing of the author, nor be otherwise circulated in any form of binding or cover other than that in which it is published and without a similar condition including this condition being imposed on the subsequent purchaser.

Edited by The Roaring Writer Ng.

Typesetting by Word2Kindle

Cover Illustrated and Designed by Rewrite Agency

Published by 'The Roaring Lion Newcastle'
ISBN: 978-1-9998159-6-7

Email:
tolu@toluakinyemi.com
author@tolutoludo.com

Website:
www.toluakinyemi.com
www.tolutoludo.com

ALSO, BY Tolu' A. Akinyemi from 'The Roaring Lion Newcastle'

"Dead Lions Don't Roar" (A collection of Poetic Wisdom for the Discerning Series 1)

"Unravel your Hidden Gems" (A collection of Inspirational and Motivational Essays)

"Dead Dogs Don't Bark" (A collection of Poetic Wisdom for the Discerning Series 2)

Dead Cats Don't Meow (A collection of Poetic Wisdom for the Discerning Series 3)

Dedication

To God Almighty, the giver of talents & gifts; He alone deserves the grace for lighting the fire of creativity in my belly & giving me the ability to put down several golden words of poetic wisdom in a 48-hour bliss, which stood the foundation for this beautiful collection, at a time I least expected my ink to flow. "THE GRAND POET, I STAN!"

Contents

Dedication — v
Acknowledgements — viii
Poems — 1

One — 2
Broken Men — 3
Petulance — 4
Hustle — 5
Finding my Feet — 6
Growth — 7
Nothing lasts forever — 8
Chocolate Skin Man — 9
Angry Poets — 10
Stigmatisation — 11
Kill me slowly — 12
Eddie — 13
Make waves — 14
Never play games with the Devil — 15

Two — 16
Western Hemisphere — 17
SARS — 18
Twitter Street — 19
RUGA — 20
Where are the cows? — 21
Northern Hemisphere — 22
The Pastor has lost his voice. — 23

Bad Governance —————————————— 24
For Asaba ——————————————————— 25
Homecoming ————————————————— 26
Eastern Hemisphere ——————————— 27
Lazy youth ——————————————————— 28
Another Precious Candle Dimmed ——— 29
Onye China ————————————————— 30
Southern Hemisphere ———————————— 31
Village People ———————————————— 32

Three ————————————————————— 33

Love Language ———————————————— 34
Sparring ——————————————————— 35
How not to woo a woman ——————— 36
Sweet for Nothing ——————————— 37
Cheating Chromosomes —————————— 38
One Woman ——————————————— 39
Rebellious ————————————————— 40
A woman's prayer. ——————————— 41
True Love —————————————————— 42
Combustible ————————————————— 43
Fly to eternity ———————————————— 44
Bio ——————————————————————— 45
Author's note ————————————————— 47

Acknowledgements

To my darling wife & partner, Olabisi, thank you for your support and listening ears on this unforeseen project. I greatly appreciate your invaluable feedback and advice.

A big thank you to my darling children, Isaac and Abigail. You both are phenomenal and priceless; you make this journey worthwhile and refreshing.

Many thanks to my ever-supportive parents. Thanks for always wrapping your arms around my shoulders and supporting me on my writing journey.

Special thanks to my editors, Gabrielina Gabriel-Abhiele and Adejuwon Gbalajobi, for their invaluable feedback and insightful ideas. Appreciation also goes to the book cover artist, Ridwan Egbeyemi, thanks for the beautiful work of art. And a massive thank you to Agboola Faith Moyosore of The African Writers for your priceless support when I needed it the most. Worthy of mention is Kolabomi Adeko for your critical review of the collection and providing some great insights. And Abi Oguntubi for never tiring of giving feedback, the words of encouragement and believing so much in my talent.

To Tayo Sangofadeji, my creative friend with the listening ear, thanks for the endless support and I'm super stoked you're also living your dreams. And to your lover, Adedotun Adebiyi I appreciate the endless support at all times.

A huge thank you to Ireti & Segun Akerele. Thanks for always having my back and giving me your total support.

A final thanks to everyone who has supported me on this journey that keeps unraveling so many booktiful experiences.

Poems

One

Tolu' A. Akinyemi

Broken Men

There are broken men whose cries are silent—
cries muted from when they became boys
& got lessons on how strong boys should be.

Men who drink from the pitfall of their mistakes
like a fountain.
Men drowning under the weight
of expectations.

Let's teach boys that they can be broken,
that they can cry and call for help
and find healing, strength and new beginnings.

Petulance

We wore labels with no trademarks
Petulant. Recalcitrant. Worthless.
Our backs had lashes tattooed on them
that became nicknames.
And some of us were tagged street boys,
we were jailed in the prison of our habits.
The Jury sent us to the hangman's noose—
no mercy.
Our youth was tainted with judgmental eyes
& tongues that set us on fire.

Hustle

Delete the excuse. Break sweat. Hustle Hard.
Hustle so hard your name won't be used as a dip-sauce
for failure in the mouth of *frenemies*.
Hustle so you won't be a corporate beggar on the streets

of social media & journey into depression when you see others
flossing.
Hustle so your missed calls won't be so pronounced on phones
of family & friends who have grown weary from giving handouts.

Hustle so you won't have a bank filled with currencies of hate—
hate at yourself for missed chances, hate for the world,
hate for family & friends with lofty houses.

Never play games with the devil

Finding my Feet

There are times we walk through these staircases that lead to nowhere—
wobbly, with unseen freckles eating deep at our confidence.
Not good enough & unfit became a parlance

mishmash into our potpourri of vocabulary.
Don't say the words expert, leader
or champion.
Keep finding your feet till you reach your Canaan.

Snatch your victory from the jaws of defeat.
Keep finding your feet until your footprints
are engraved on the sands of time.

Think broken chords & mangled bodies
defeated in the canvas of your mind.

Tolu' A. Akinyemi

Growth

See life from the spectacles of growth.
We live. We grow. We don't stop learning.
Don't hold back, live free & intentional —
unravel all your hidden gems & diamonds.

Even more-so, glow!
You are a work in progress, an unfinished article.
Write your name out in gold. Be bold.

Don't come to the parade ground lax,
the pity-party host in my neighborhood was a no-show.
Show up, audition for it, just do it.

Nothing lasts forever

You say poverty knows your name & being piss-poor
is your lot.
I tell you, life is so unpredictable like Manchester's weather—
rain one-minute, intense sunlight the next.

You have been imprisoned by the cobwebs of life,
in a circle of unending poverty. Will this ever change?
You have questions upon questions
but the answers are not in sight.

I say nothing lasts forever
Scatter your seeds,
you never know which might yield a bountiful harvest.
Delete negative vibes
& jump those high walls first in your mind.

Keep hope, keep buzzing with hope
till you see a new horizon.

Tolu' A. Akinyemi

Chocolate Skin Man

Wearing my skin like a hard nut & a tough cookie.
I wore my dreams on my sleeve—
chocolate skin does not crack.

Show them that melanin is the new gold,
chocolate is another name for beauty.
Don't delete the brains.

Mélange in caramel dripping hot, hot,
& all its shades.
Revel in the colour of this skin, nourish it

chocolate skin does not tan & fade.
Sing this tune so loud, the Chocolate skin man is
self-made.

Never play games with the devil

Angry Poets

I have an arsenal of metaphors to show my anger
There are days I cry tears mixed with pain & anger.
I listen to the news & I'm angry. Instagram drives me to rage.
There is enough bad news to last a lifetime!

They call us angry poets,
angry about the injustice that walks fearless on our streets.
Give me a shirt with the inscription screaming ***angry poet.***
Angry poet is a hyperbole conjured in the mind for a soft landing..

The more injustice, the more my anger burns
like a fiery furnace.

Stigmatisation

Drown the voices of imperfection
It's okay to be imperfect. It's okay to stutter & stammer
& be like a TV with no signal.
She is too short! He is too thin! He is ugly! She is fat!

Lose some weight! Shed that fat!
Don't rain on someone else's parade.
There are times we adorn labels
that don't fit to strangers & friends alike.

We bury dreams, strength, taking away the fortitude to forge on.
We kill hope in its bloom &
wilt because of stigma.

Never play games with the devil

Kill me slowly

This is how to kill my self-confidence:

Tell me all the exploits my mates have accomplished,
how the son of the short man next door has been called to the
Bar,
not like me, jumping from bar to bar in London.

Tell me of my mate who went to the moon
& kissed the sun. Don't forget the one who
built a mansion on Mars.

Tell me one at a time.
Blurt the words till I freak out
& my life becomes a blur.

Tolu' A. Akinyemi

Eddie

There are names that carry stigmas,
heads that bring shame—
say Eddie, Edmund, Edward...
then you think of boys with a burden for head,
boys being slaughtered by the tongue of peers.
These are boys who spend their youths fighting for survival,
fighting the voices of mockers,
mocking them for head-shapes they didn't choose.

Make waves

I want to make waves like CNA.
Have my name amongst elite African voices on CNN.
Think legacies, say Usain Bolt.
I watch webinars on one thousand and one ways
to become a bestselling author.
I'm a house with different rooms: Poetry & Prose.
I'm a human with a foreign body,
A tree with several roots.

My brain thinks faster than my words can convey.
My mind works magic. Can I live this life forever?

Tolu' A. Akinyemi

Never play games with the Devil

They say never with the devil play games
For he will drown you like the River Thames
Never you with the devil roll dice
He'd make you lose as much twice
The devil plays a three-dimensional chess
Playing fair with him is but useless
He'd leave you clueless & trading blames

Never with the devil make a pact
He will ask for an arm & a leg & a heart
Give you a wheelchair & collect the wheels
Put you on slippery grounds and give you heels
And your sorrow will be copious as morning dew
For He'd ask ten times more what is due
Leaving you playing blame games

When you see the devil from yonder
Flee, run, for he only wants to take you under
When Life happens, and the devil brings a deal
Run, Flee, for he'd make you eat woe for a meal
Never you play games with the devil
Not even mind games for he's pure evil
Just confuse him with his numbers, & beat him at his mind games.

Two

Tolu' A. Akinyemi

Western Hemisphere

They say never play with a lion's tail,
for you might not live to tell the story.
The nomads tow the path of ruin.

Send back these insipid wanderers back to the far ends.
They don't belong here,
on our farms, killing our people.
Send them back to Chad, Mali & Niger,
to whatever holes they crawled out from

Don't provoke *Oduduwa* with the drumbeats of war. I say don't.
Don't tickle a sleeping tiger, I say this without punctuations
nevereveryoudaretrespassinthewesternhemisphere.

Never play games with the devil

SARS

Yahoo! Shhhhh! Let no one utter those abominable words here.
In this city with no rules
Everyone is a suspect.
This stethoscope is used to fish out yahoo boys.

Our streets are blood-stained
The innocent pummelled with bullets
SARS is a metaphor for gruesome killers!

The binocular of SARS is on the look-out
for tattoos—
No good boy wears a tattoo.
In this city with no laws
Fear SARS the way you fear death.

SARS is an acronym for Special Anti-Robbery Squad, a branch of the Nigeria Police Force under the Force Criminal Investigation and Intelligence Department (FCIID).

Tolu' A. Akinyemi

Twitter Street

Don't make me trend on Twitter street
for reasons not noble.
Don't carry my name like a banner so high,
then bring me down like a pack of falling cards.

I will bury my ignorance in my back garden
to avoid my name being chewed upon by strangers.
Think, think twice before you tweet those words
that stink of reputation damage.

Lest malfeasance of your old tweets is announced on
the day your name is announced on the news for a worthy cause.
The stench shall be blown by the east wind to the west end,
then you will know that this twitter street
is not a playground for the faint hearted.

Never play games with the devil

RUGA

RUGA this
RUGA that
Talk sleeping leaders who wake up to buffoonery.
Shift left. Shift Right. Shift your RUGA to Sambisa!

RUGA your confusion back to the North,
drown it in the deepest part of the Niger!
Sail. Sail RUGA to where the Niger meets Benue
Build a home for your Ruga in the bottomless pit.

RUGA the harbingers of confusion
& their paymasters
to the land of no return.

RUGA is an acronym for Rural Grazing Area and it also means human settlement. RUGA is a policy proposed by the Federal Government of Nigeria to give Land in every state of the federation to Fulani herdsmen as an antidote to the incessant killings of farmers and kidnapping of the citizenry.

Tolu' A. Akinyemi

Where are the cows?

Sycophancy turned grown men into clowns,
no stage, just a mic and a voice to spill bucket loads of gibberish.
When dreams fizzled
& an old man was wailing.

You mean there were no cows,
no trace?
Whose account do we believe?
It can't be men with solid colored shirts,

they are saints, they are without blemish,
spotless, without sin.
Let's kill truth on the altar of ambition & politics.

It can't be the nomads. Wait let me make a guess,
they must be kidnappers & armed robbers
Unless you show me the cows.

Never play games with the devil

Northern Hemisphere

Write North a letter not to turn a blind eye.
Why North? Why turn a blind eye to the failings of your kinsmen?
Man, with the good luck was *a scapegoat*
some say, banter & served as toast.

Write North a letter sent via Lugard's graveyard.
My eyes are made teary by this amalgamation of woes.
They choke,
they choke from their silence.

Write North a letter they have failed woefully
Write to the North, maybe they will get it right
before they're consumed by the inferno of silence.

Tolu' A. Akinyemi

The Pastor has lost his voice.

Election rigging, ballot snatching, and herdsmen killings,
the pastor looks away.
Tell Jesus this task is herculean,
the path of honour is hard to take.

You see exaggerated killings, I see bloodbath,
I see clueless men in the corridors of power
I see a pastor who has lost his way.
Give us a national minister of mourning.

Never say errand boy, star boy divides opinion.
I see filth, I see dollars in Kano,
I see bigotry, ethnicity, a cabal-controlled government
& a pastor who has lost his voice.

Never play games with the devil

Bad Governance

You scream bad governance but I have a different viewpoint.
You have a notepad littered with all the flaws of this government with a penchant for breaking laws.
Before the elections, we saw voltrons & internet monsters
who hid behind those sacred keypads
to showcase the achievements of their paymasters.
Before you mourn and throw tantrums
about the next level of bad governance, look into this dingy magic mirror.

Who do you see? Yourself!
Hold yourself to account for gallantly walking into a ditch
with your eyes wide-opened before you scream
bad governance.

Tolu' A. Akinyemi

For Asaba

This is for Asaba & our short-lived love.
Maybe the Author in me would have been **under construction**
if I hadn't chosen to break up our affair
before I bloomed into a nine-to-five hustler

& wear a pan-Nigerian hat that didn't fit.
Asaba was a land of lessons with no curriculum—
a city that harbored dreams like a loaded ship on the dockyard.

Don't wipe out these chapters from my pages
Never erase this episode from my series of soap operas
for the outcome will be torn pages.
Let me write this love poem to Asaba—
a vital part of my becoming.

Homecoming

Every time I ponder on homecoming, my mind wanders into a dreamland
I see a caricature democrat who can never wipe the name **"dictator"**
tattooed on his chest like a visible lamp post in an unlit street.

Every time I contemplate on homecoming, I hear voices saying arrest him,
arrest that poet, that Writer who uses the pen to throw shit at us.
My mind ruminates, who fears death?
We will all heed this glorious call someday.

Every time I ruminate on homecoming, I say a prayer too much:
I pray for light, water & the grace to see another day.
I pray against being a scapegoat to an unscrupulous police officer
who might just shoot the wrong shot.

Every time I reflect on homecoming,
I pray against being caught in the web
of kidnappers, armed-robbers &
the nest of the notorious Fulani herdsmen.

The menace of Boko Haram deserves its own book!
Homecoming is synonymous with more prayers.
Don't ask me why I fear homecoming.

Tolu' A. Akinyemi

Eastern Hemisphere

They sing the songs of war,
dust their British passport & run for safety.
Camouflage under the radar of sectionalism
the beast from the east has run out of steam,
hot today, colder than ice in the morrow.

The wind from the East screams industrialisation,
"Look here, we don't do idleness.
"Lazy youths don't have a place here."

Lazy youth

Colour us with a crayon on a white cardboard paper
with the tag "lazy youth".
Publish abroad our failings & incompetence.

Don't refute those words that came out pristine
from your oesophagus on the altar of fake news.

There are no lazy youths in this clime,
maybe lazy public servants who brazenly display wealth
they could not in good faith work for in this life & the one after.

The lazy youths fight for survival, they tread this lonely path with
no help.

The government snores away in intermittent slumber,
caught in the web of ineptitude and failing infrastructure.

Lazy youths are a mirage of monumental proportions
concocted by the certificate-less man.

Tolu' A. Akinyemi

Another Precious Candle Dimmed

(For Precious Owolabi)

Every protest is an occasion for bloodbath
No city is exempted.
I say the federal capital, even Aso Rock,
is not exempted.

Another Precious corper kissed the dust.
Somewhere in Kaduna, a family is mourning—
their precious boy is gone.

The nation seats majestic on a keg of gunpowder,
we are on a knife edge.
There are cities where human lives are worthless,
where the sting of death festers like an open sore.

Never play games with the devil

Onye China

Stop chasing clout
Your blessings will come
Don't **cum** before you hear the revival song

Gather those stones & build castles
This is not a break or make up story
To whet our appetite with make believe tales

It might cause tears & blood
The dark clouds gather
We saw it rain pain & hurt.
Don't be a lead actor in a faux pas movie

The winds blew *onye from China*
 to halt the madness of a fake blessing.

Tolu' A. Akinyemi

Southern Hemisphere

In the Southern Hemisphere, the rivers flow with oil
Our fishes are stillborn
They took our oil, our dreams & hopes
So we can't toil.

Think poverty & affluence
A few moneybags & our youths wrapped in body bags
Farmlands become waste places
The farms have become alien to plants & crops.
Oil soiled our land & hands—
say barren lands & waste places.

The goose that lays the golden eggs
is in a *melancholy*,
A perpetual state of *inertia*
caused by the *sidon look* attitude of the sons of the soil.

Never play games with the devil

Village People

In those hinterlands called villages are people—
humans that fly at night,
ragged mothers of the night.

They ease through walls like they don't exist,
they see no borders, they require no visa.
I see village people— principalities & night marauders.
Mon Pere says with heaviness felt in the weight of his words.

Hide, hide your blessings from village people
before they bring you down like a plane blown into pieces
with a missile.
I'm thinking. Thinking aloud. How can I hide?
I laminate my blessings & take a screenshot.

Don't ask me why I pray, why I take the Communion,
why I pray without ceasing.
My village people are coming,
but they are coming to their end.

Three

Love Language

There is no university where they take courses in love languages
Affection has no undertone, it's either love or love,
Forget the connotations of lust.
There is a language that conquers all

Dive deep and submerge yourself under its currents.
A little hug, words of affirmation can heal a troubled soul
Quality time spent together can fire up a loveless union.
Immerse yourself in love, chew on its languages,
let love find you from the four corners of the earth.

Tolu' A. Akinyemi

Sparring

We were sparring & warring
Our armory was filled with vile words.
We threw fisticuffs without fists,
just darts of words sharpened with hate.

I sent a mail in the letterbox with no words
I wore silence on my fluffy cheeks like a blush.

Don't break the table
& smash it into pieces,
when there's no perfect human.
They say time heals all wounds, a week after, maybe two,
Time will join the broken pieces together.

No one would see the leak— we perfume our filth
& start a new journey.

Never play games with the devil

How not to woo a woman

There are men whose words can't hold water with a woman
Give me a manual on how to woo a woman
& I will give you orchards with blooming hibiscus.

There are men whose legs wobble when they see love
Who says you can't be disabled in the mind?
There are men who stutter when they see beauty—
Love struck stammers.

I'm on the look-out for a woman crush
A woman unabashed
That's the easiest route to my destination
On how not to woo a woman.

Tolu' A. Akinyemi

Sweet for Nothing

We say so many words that are sweet-for-nothing
Too many **attention-grabbing** words eroded with the passage of time.

We build a home on the sand with strangers
from the foundations of emptiness & sweet-for-nothings.

We are trapped in the web of promises, false promises
that soon evaporate when the veil of deceit is broken.
Sing me a song from the heart— your heart.

Hold me by the hand on this journey
to a city that does not crumble.

Cheating Chromosomes

Bury my cheating chromosomes in the sand
& draw a heart over it.
I will drink from your cistern till your water runs dry
& I thirst no more.

Mini-stroke was the lot of Kamoru,
the one whose wife parted her legs
like the Red Sea to a ragged stranger.
How do you prepare to check the phone of a cheating partner?
Never, don't ever dare!

Notes from the writing-pad of a cheating partner
makes the heart beat at an electric pace,
blood pumping like a car at neck-speed pace.
Take the first exit to the shower,
say a little prayer
& purge all your cheating chromosomes one at a time.

Tolu' A. Akinyemi

One Woman

Teach me to love one woman till my bones grow frail
& my skin wrinkles.
They say more money more problems.
I retort, 'More women, more troubles!'

Teach me to dance with one woman,
teach me to dance to her song alone
till death do us part.

Rebellious

You see a rebellious woman,
I see a confident woman.
Those words have become trite
 to use on this precious egghead.

Today we squabble,
Tomorrow we become inseparable like five and six.
They say love endures all weather,
 I carry the banner high, no buts, what ifs or maybes'.

I will take this walk over and over again
with this rebellious woman till we find our way to paradise.

Tolu' A. Akinyemi

A woman's prayer.

We win wars without uttering words.
We don't crash under the weight of the world
on our shoulders like a bushed weightlifter.

A woman's prayer is powerful—
think mothers with babies strapped around their backs
in church vigil.
A praying woman can do the impossible!

A praying wife makes a union without strife,
she is armed with wisdom and gentleness,
and her prayers open doors to a life of victory.

True Love

Give me true love
Open your arms wide & engulf me in the flames of love
Don't let the chasm of our childhood separate us.

Spread your wings & fly
I will be by your side
Let me be your cheerleader, you can be the Hero.

Let's build a home together in love's paradise
Let true love be the song on our lips
Love me at full tilt with love untainted.

Tolu' A. Akinyemi

Combustible

She was loving & doting
when love was at the nucleus.
She hid my name in the innermost part of her heart
and built a temple for me as a remembrance.

Our names submerged in the ocean & could not be drowned.
She was a goddess to be worshipped, revered.
She was fury & combustible,
a little spark & she is on fire.

Killing memories, beautiful memories,
our love became a memoriam.

Never play games with the devil

Fly to eternity

Let's fly this plane with no stopovers to eternity
Boeing Cruise on Auto-Pilot to Love Island.
You said love is a hoax,
I reply, "You have not found the one
who completes you."

I will build you a house on solid grounds
& parachute you sheltered in my arms to high heavens,
till we land secure in eternity.

Fly baby,
Fly with me to eternity.

bio

Tolu' Akinyemi is an exceptional talent, out-of-the box creative thinker; a change management agent and a leader par excellence. Tolu' is a business analyst and financial crime consultant as well as a Certified Anti-Money Laundering Specialist (CAMS) with extensive experience working with leading Investment Banks and Consultancy Firms. Tolu' is also a personal development and career coach and a prolific writer with more than 10 years' writing experience. He is a mentor to hundreds of young people. He worked as an Associate Mentor in St Mary's School, Cheshunt and as an Inclusion Mentor in Barnwell School, Stevenage in the United Kingdom, helping students raise their aspirations, standards of performance and helping them cope with transitions from one educational stage to another.

A man whom many refer to as "Mr Vision", he is a trained Economist from Ekiti State University formerly known as University of Ado-Ekiti (UNAD). He sat his Masters' Degree in Accounting and Financial Management at the University of Hertfordshire, Hatfield, United Kingdom. Tolu' was a student ambassador at the University of Hertfordshire, Hatfield representing the University in major forums and engaging with young people during various assignments.

Tolu' Akinyemi is a home-grown talent; an alumnus of the Daystar Leadership Academy (DLA), he is passionate about people and wealth creation. He believes so much that life is about impacting on others. In his words, "To have a Secure Future, we must be willing to pay the Price in order to earn the Prize".

Tolu' has headlined and featured in various Poetry Festivals, Open Slam, Poetry Slam, Spoken Word and Open Mic events in and outside the United Kingdom. He also inspires large audiences through spoken word performances, he has appeared as a keynote speaker in major forums and events and facilitates creative writing masterclasses to all types of audiences.

Tolu' Akinyemi was born in Ado-Ekiti, Nigeria and currently lives in the United Kingdom. Tolu' is an ardent supporter of Chelsea Football Club, London.

You can connect with Tolu' on his various Social Media Accounts:

Instagram: @tolutoludo
Facebook: facebook.com/toluaakinyemi
Twitter: @toluakinyemi

author's note

Thank you for the time you have taken to read this book. I hope you enjoyed the poems in it.

If you loved the book and have a minute to spare, I would appreciate a short review on the page or site where you bought the book. I greatly appreciate your help in spreading the word. Reviews from readers like you make a huge difference to helping new readers get the book.

Thank you!

Tolu' Akinyemi

www.ingramcontent.com/pod-product-compliance
Lightning Source LLC
Chambersburg PA
CBHW020548080526
44583CB00013B/1058